666

666

THE MARK OF THE BEAST MADE SIMPLE

DR. PATRICK OBEN

Deshen
Publishing the Word

ISBN: 978-1-7320297-6-7

TABLE OF CONTENTS

DEDICATION

To the Holy Spirit, who opens my eyes to see Jesus in the Bible

INTRODUCTION

The mysterious number 666 and the dreaded mark of the beast have long captured the imaginations of millions. Demystifying their meanings can help Christians navigate our rapidly changing world more effectively.

Many Christians struggle to understand 666 and the mark of the beast because of the complexity of the book of Revelation, diverse theological perspectives, and a multitude of speculative theories. This confusion can lead to anxiety and fear, highlighting the importance of providing believers with a clear and concise understanding of these concepts.

Despite these challenges, Christians can clearly understand 666 and the mark of the beast, with proper guidance. This understanding can bring many benefits, including increased stability and a sense of calm amid the chaos of the world. Additionally, they can avoid being tossed around by the waves of various predictions about the mark of the beast. I wrote this book to provide such an understanding—a clear and accessible explanation of 666 that is theologically sound, and free of complex details or guesswork.

In this book, readers will learn that 666 is a number derived from symbolic numerology that identifies the Antichrist, and that the mark of the beast is ultimately a spiritual symbol representing allegiance to the Antichrist, though it has a physical expression. By the end, readers will have a solid understanding of 666 and the mark of the beast and be able to approach the subject confidently without being confused by ambiguous ideas or being swayed by obscure speculations.

To present this key message simply, clearly, and concisely, I have meticulously scrutinized relevant theological texts, drawing on my years of studying and teaching the Bible, as well as my analytical precision as a physician. I have distilled the material into the essential truths, which I have explained in this book. I deliberately avoided getting into an in-depth theological analysis of Revelation, 666, or the mark of the beast. Additionally, I did not write this book to predict the year of Jesus's second coming, the Antichrist's identity, or the actual mark of the beast.

So if you are ready to understand 666 simply and clearly within an hour or two, let's embark on this fascinating journey together. We will start by providing a foundation for properly understanding the number and the mark without guesswork.

CONTEXTUALIZING 666 AND THE MARK OF THE BEAST

The key to understanding 666 and the mark of the beast can be found in examining the biblical, historical, and end-times context of Revelation 13:16–18, the pivotal passage for this topic.

BIBLICAL CONTEXT

The number 666 appears only three times in the Bible. The most well-known instance is in Revelation 13:18:

> *"This calls for wisdom: let the one who has understanding calculate the number of the beast, for it is the number of a man, and his number is 666."*
>
> (REVELATION 13:18, ESV)

Interestingly, the other two occurrences are connected to Solomon, who received 666 talents of gold each year (1

Kings 10:14; 2 Chronicles 9:13). Connecting Solomon's life to the end-times 666 would be a bold and inventive speculation. While the rationale remains uncertain, that Solomon's annual gold income is the only other mention of 666 in the Bible is likely not coincidental.

Unlike 666, the phrase "mark of the beast" is exclusive to the Book of Revelation. Nonetheless, we can find a related idea in Ezekiel 9:4, where God instructs an angel in a prophetic vision to journey through Jerusalem and set a mark upon the foreheads of those who grieve and mourn over the city's sins.

A thorough understanding of how these concepts appear in the Bible is crucial, as is recognizing the historical period in which it was written.

HISTORICAL CONTEXT

Most scholars believe John wrote the Book of Revelation around AD 95–96, during the reign of Domitian, the Roman Emperor.

During the first century AD, the early Christian Church faced immense persecution under the reigns of Emperor Nero and Emperor Domitian. In AD 70, the Romans destroyed Jerusalem, fulfilling Jesus's prophecy about the end times, as detailed in Matthew 24:1–2. These challenging events significantly shaped the early church and provided the context for the book of Revelation.

Apocalyptic writings like the Book of Revelation often emerge during times of severe distress. These texts use symbolic language and imagery to convey messages of hope and divine intervention for believers.

Understanding the historical context is essential because the first readers of John's letter (Revelation) would have interpreted his message based on their contemporary circumstances and culture. To understand Revelation nearly 2000 years later, we must strive to comprehend it as the first readers did.

These early Christians lived under conditions similar to those described in Revelation, under Rome's rule, the fourth empire in Daniel's visions and in Nebuchadnezzar's dream. Thus, when they read John's Revelation, they related his message to their current situation (Rome) and past experiences (Babylon, Medo-Persia, Greece). However, John's message about 666 and the mark of the beast extends beyond their time, pointing to the end times.

Figure 1 illustrates how the history of Babylon and Rome foreshadows future events.

Figure 1: Essential Historical Precedents Leading to the Antichrist's Global Governance

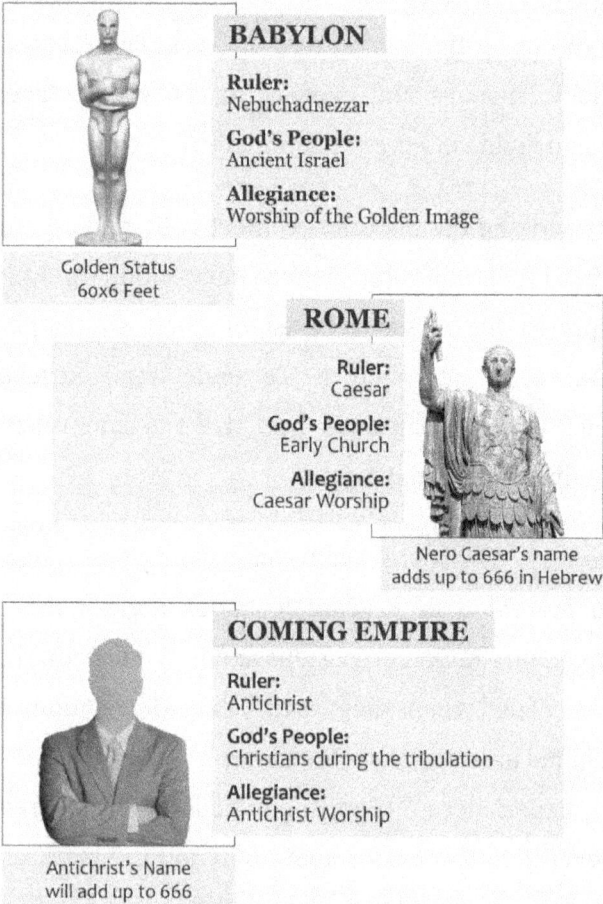

BABYLON

Ruler:
Nebuchadnezzar

God's People:
Ancient Israel

Allegiance:
Worship of the Golden Image

Golden Status
60x6 Feet

ROME

Ruler:
Caesar

God's People:
Early Church

Allegiance:
Caesar Worship

Nero Caesar's name
adds up to 666 in Hebrew

COMING EMPIRE

Ruler:
Antichrist

God's People:
Christians during the tribulation

Allegiance:
Antichrist Worship

Antichrist's Name
will add up to 666

We are witnessing events that align with the end times, as prophesied by Jesus in Matthew 24. Unlike the early Christians, we have the historical context of all four empires from Daniel's visions and Nebuchadnezzar's dream: Babylon, Medo-Persia, Greece, and Rome. Furthermore, the Scriptures still point to the future arrival of the ultimate Antichrist and a global empire.

END-TIMES CONTEXT

History, from Babylon to Rome, and events since Rome's fall provide glimpses into what God had said about the end times, through the prophets. Each generation since Rome's fall can observe this divine narrative and recognize aspects of what is coming.

The end times will bring dramatic circumstances to the earth, and God has outlined the key people, places, events, and timelines in His word, written thousands of years in advance. Figure 2 highlights some significant themes and events during the end times.

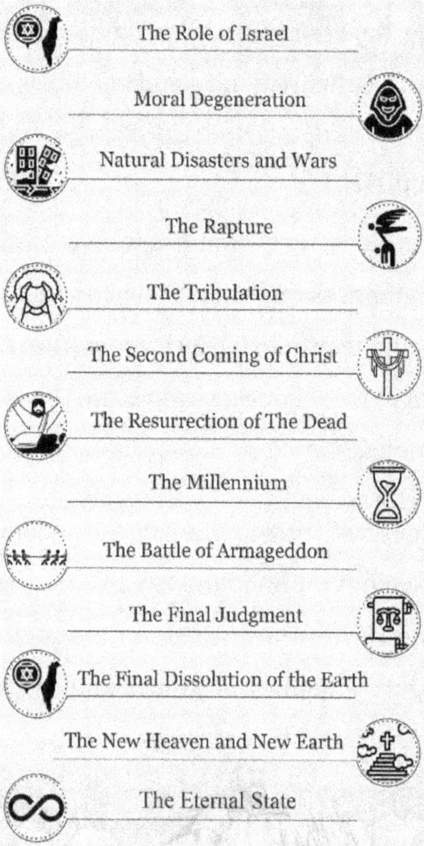

Figure 2: Major Themes of **End Times Events**

(Events not in strict order)

The Role of Israel

Moral Degeneration

Natural Disasters and Wars

The Rapture

The Tribulation

The Second Coming of Christ

The Resurrection of The Dead

The Millennium

The Battle of Armageddon

The Final Judgment

The Final Dissolution of the Earth

The New Heaven and New Earth

The Eternal State

In this end-times narrative, a significant scene featuring 666 and the mark of the beast emerges. The following key elements of this scene, illustrated in Figure 3, are essential for understanding its context and implications:

- The Dragon - Satan
- The Beast from the sea - the Antichrist
- The Beast from the land - the False Prophet
- The empire or worldwide kingdom
- The image of the Antichrist
- The name of the Antichrist
- The number of the name of the Antichrist (666)
- The mark of the beast
- Worship
- Worshippers of the Beast
- Worshippers of Christ

Figure 3: Pivotal Components of the
Era of the Antichrist's Rule

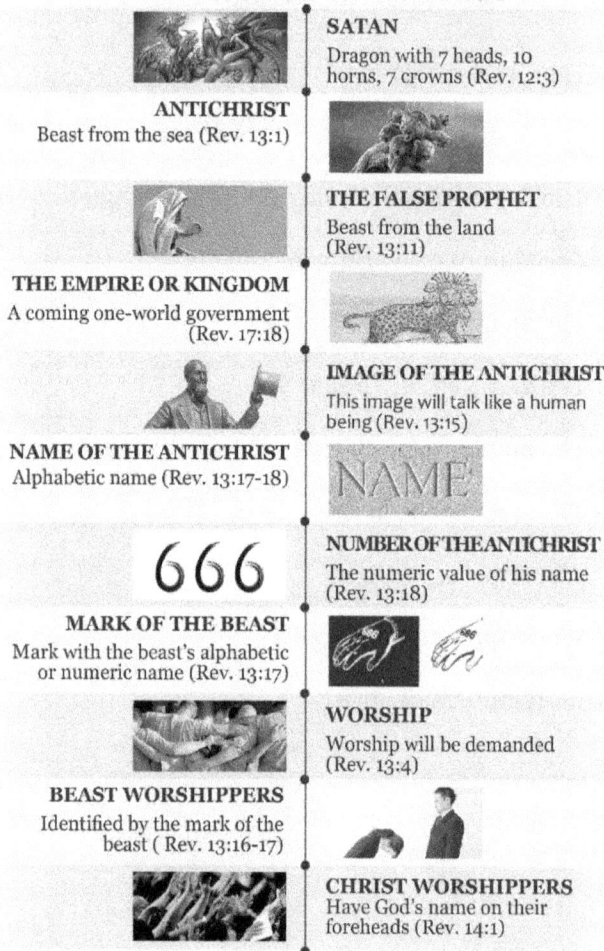

SATAN
Dragon with 7 heads, 10 horns, 7 crowns (Rev. 12:3)

ANTICHRIST
Beast from the sea (Rev. 13:1)

THE FALSE PROPHET
Beast from the land (Rev. 13:11)

THE EMPIRE OR KINGDOM
A coming one-world government (Rev. 17:18)

IMAGE OF THE ANTICHRIST
This image will talk like a human being (Rev. 13:15)

NAME OF THE ANTICHRIST
Alphabetic name (Rev. 13:17-18)

NUMBER OF THE ANTICHRIST
The numeric value of his name (Rev. 13:18)

666

MARK OF THE BEAST
Mark with the beast's alphabetic or numeric name (Rev. 13:17)

WORSHIP
Worship will be demanded (Rev. 13:4)

BEAST WORSHIPPERS
Identified by the mark of the beast (Rev. 13:16-17)

CHRIST WORSHIPPERS
Have God's name on their foreheads (Rev. 14:1)

666 AND THE MARK OF THE BEAST IN CONTEXT

The proper context—biblical, historical, and eschatological—serves as the foundation for understanding 666 and the mark of the beast. As demonstrated above, the essential elements of this context are relatively straightforward. The rest of the book will be similarly accessible.

I have intentionally avoided detailing each item to maintain the book's conciseness. I encourage readers to consult additional resources to explore any themes further if they feel the need before continuing.

With the foundation laid, we can now place the first block to build our understanding of 666 and the mark of the beast. This first step involves demystifying the book of Revelation, which contains these concepts. Many Christians might prefer to avoid this mysterious biblical book, but after reading the next chapter, "Navigating the Unknown: Demystifying Revelation Without Guesswork," you'll discover that, with proper guidance, Christians can both understand and enjoy reading this enigmatic book.

DEMYSTIFYING REVELATION WITHOUT GUESSWORK

Is it possible for ordinary Christians, without formal training in prophecy, eschatology, or apocalyptic writings, to truly grasp the mysterious concepts of 666 and the mark of the beast?

In the previous chapter, we laid the foundation for proper context—biblical, historical, and eschatological. In this chapter, you will learn that any Christian can understand Revelation, with proper guidance and without becoming entangled in age-old theological controversies or never-ending end-time prophecy speculations.

REVELATION: AN ACCESSIBLE BOOK

John addressed the book of Revelation to the Christians in the seven local churches in Asia Minor, expecting all the believers would understand his message, regardless of their theological expertise. He did not directly address his letter to Jewish rabbis, experts in Jewish law, or those skilled in apocalyptic writings.

However, John's call for wisdom in Revelation 13:18 implies that understanding 666 and the mark of the beast demands greater insight than the average person had in his day. In this book, I provide straightforward guidance that will equip readers with the essential skills to navigate the complexities of 666 confidently.

ACKNOWLEDGING REVELATION'S COMPLEXITY

In stating that Christians without special theological training can understand the book of Revelation, I do not intend to undermine the complexity of this book. The book of Revelation is undoubtedly one of the most complex books in the Bible. This complexity implies that we should keep two crucial points in mind as we proceed:

1. We should acknowledge and respect the reality that some passages are difficult to understand. God, in His infinite wisdom, has intentionally used symbolic

language to conceal certain truths in that book until the end.

2. Because some passages and concepts are unclear, Christians have different perspectives about what they mean. Consequently, we should have a healthy respect for these differing perspectives. In this book, we will focus on the aspects that are clear and identify areas with differing viewpoints as needed.

Despite this complexity and ambiguity, there are some common pitfalls we should avoid.

PITFALLS TO AVOID

Here are three common errors, framed as guidelines, that we must avoid as we seek to understand 666 and the mark of the beast:

1. Do not attempt to identify the Antichrist before the time God has set for him to be revealed to the world. Any attempt to use 666 to identify who the Antichrist is will probably fail, so it is best to steer clear of it. When the Antichrist comes onto the world stage and becomes the worldwide political leader, he will be

recognized as such, and the meaning and application of 666 will make perfect sense to those equipped with the knowledge shared in this book.

2. Do not seek to predict what the mark of the beast will be before its time. When the beast (the Antichrist) is known, the mark of the beast will be clear to all.

3. Do not seek to know what God has concealed until the appointed time. As a master communicator, God has concealed some truths only to be revealed in the last days. For instance, if God has purposefully withheld the exact year of Jesus's return (which Jesus Himself said he did not know), do not seek to predict it or listen to anyone who claims to know it.

If we avoid these three pitfalls, we can use the tools at our disposal to understand what God wants us to know without the pressure of having to be exact.

AIDS TO INTERPRETATION

Christians in A.D. 95–96 understood Revelation readily, just as most people today are familiar with smartphones. To understand Revelation today, it is essential to read it as the Christians in the seven churches who received John's letter did. For this, we need help from experts to bridge the wide gap between us, including cultural, linguistic, and historical differences.

An exhaustive treatment of the aids to understanding Revelation is beyond the scope of this book. Instead, we will focus on three things that will help us, especially concerning 666 and the mark of the beast:

1. Context is crucial. In Chapter 1, we discussed the biblical, historical, and eschatological context of Revelation 13:18.

2. Symbolism is key. Symbolic language is central to prophecy and apocalyptic writings. God often uses symbols to represent people, places, events, or things in visions shown to prophets. For example, John saw the Antichrist as a beast emerging from the sea, a symbol representing a man. Grasping this concept of symbolism puts us well on our way toward understanding the mark of the beast.

3. First steps matter. Begin your interpretation on solid ground; start with what is clear, then proceed to the ambiguous. One of the best clues to understanding what 666 or the mark means is to look for similar passages in Revelation or other biblical books that speak to similar concepts with more clarity. For example, God's seal or name on His people's forehead (Revelation 14:1) is a vital interpretative clue.

An additional aid involves questions that help us understand symbolic language:

TWO CRUCIAL QUESTIONS ABOUT SYMBOLS

Understanding symbols is crucial for interpreting Revelation. Here are two questions we must seek to answer about 666 and the mark of the beast (please see Figure 4):

1. Is the mark of the beast a symbol that stands for something else, or is it a literal bodily mark in real life?

2. If it is a symbol, the next question is, what does the symbol represent?

Figure 4: Two Crucial Questions for Unraveling
Symbolism in Revelation

Symbol Vs Reality

Is what I am reading symbolic or the actual thing? Figurative or literal?

Decoding Symbols

If it's a symbol, what does it stand for?

666

With the foundation of proper context and the first step in navigating Revelation, the drama is about to begin. In our next chapter, we delve into one of the most intriguing and significant aspects of end-times prophecy: the Antichrist and the rise of a global empire.

THE ANTICHRIST AND THE RISE OF A GLOBAL EMPIRE

I magine a world where every move is monitored, and a single mark signifies loyalty to a Satanic ruler. Welcome to the era of the Antichrist and the mark of the beast.

With the proper understanding of the context and perspective on Revelation, we shift our focus to a world where 666 and the mark become as commonplace as smartphones today. In this new order, the Antichrist spearheads a worldwide government, unleashing chaos and destruction on Earth. We'll first examine the man, then his worldwide empire.

THE TERM "ANTICHRIST"

John mentions multiple antichrists in his writing, making it a valid question to ask which one he was referring to in Revelation 13:18.

The term "antichrist" appears only four times in the Bible, all by John in his epistles (1 Jn. 2:18, 22; 4:3; 2 Jn. 7), but the concept occurs elsewhere: Beast from the sea (Rev. 13:1); the man of lawlessness (2 Th. 2:3–9); coming prince (Daniel 6:26); or little horn (Daniel 7:8). The term could mean "against Christ" or "in place of Christ."

John's use of "antichrist" in his epistles and Revelation conveys a broader meaning as understood by Christians in his time:

1. People denying Jesus as Christ (1 John 2:18, 22; 2 John 7), resulting in many antichrists—past and present.

2. The spirit of the antichrist, the animating force producing the antichrist attitude in people, is already here and working.

3. The Antichrist, a man John saw as a monstrous beast emerging from the sea in a symbolic vision, is still to come.

For our purposes, the Antichrist we are concerned about is a specific individual, a man who will become a worldwide ruler.

THE ANTICHRIST

The Antichrist will emerge as a human political ruler, ascending to power and governing a one-world system. He will have a name symbolically represented by 666 and implement a method to identify his adherents—the mark of the beast.

The Bible provides only a sketch of this identity without revealing explicit details. As you now know, we should respect the limits of knowledge imposed in the Bible; we should stop where God stops and not attempt to know or explain what God has concealed until the appointed time.

With this in mind, understanding the Antichrist is crucial to understanding 666 and the mark. If the Antichrist were to present himself and his qualifications, his profile would likely resemble the description outlined in Figure 5.

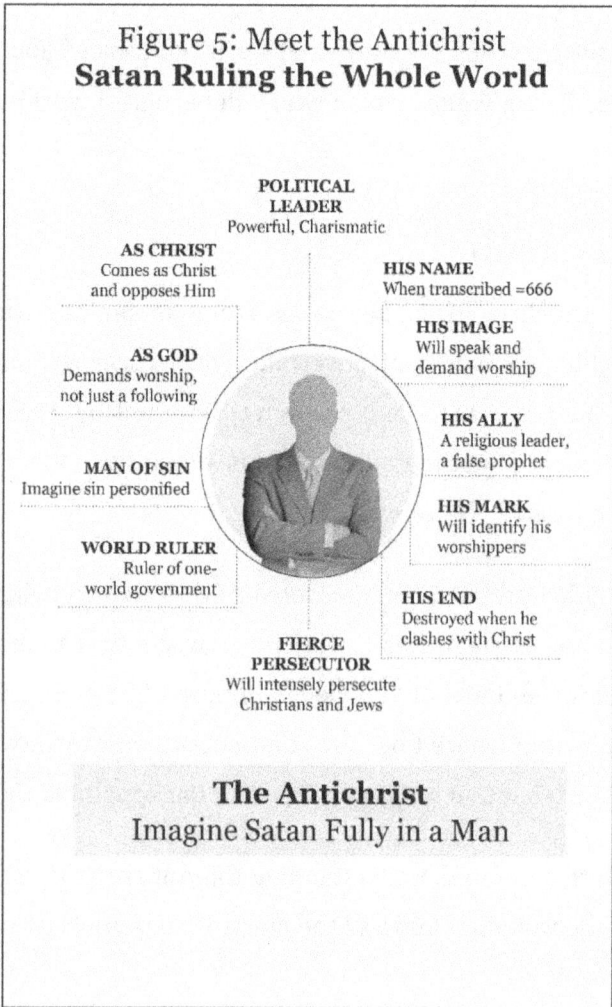

Figure 5: Meet the Antichrist
Satan Ruling the Whole World

POLITICAL LEADER
Powerful, Charismatic

AS CHRIST
Comes as Christ
and opposes Him

HIS NAME
When transcribed =666

HIS IMAGE
Will speak and
demand worship

AS GOD
Demands worship,
not just a following

HIS ALLY
A religious leader,
a false prophet

MAN OF SIN
Imagine sin personified

HIS MARK
Will identify his
worshippers

WORLD RULER
Ruler of one-
world government

HIS END
Destroyed when he
clashes with Christ

FIERCE PERSECUTOR
Will intensely persecute
Christians and Jews

The Antichrist
Imagine Satan Fully in a Man

THE GLOBAL EMPIRE OR GOVERNMENT

During the Antichrist's reign, the mark of the beast will serve as a government-imposed identification to distinguish those who worship the Antichrist (the beast). It will be a global government ID in a forthcoming new world order that grants special privileges to those who bear the mark and imposes severe restrictions on those who don't.

Remember that this new world is not imaginary or visionary; it will be the real world we know today under different circumstances. Upon examining world events, one can see that they are rapidly changing to fulfill this end-time prophecy. A new world is approaching in which routine tasks, like buying groceries or selling something online, will require a specific ID—the mark of the beast.

THE BEAST AND HIS BEASTLY EMPIRE

The Antichrist and his government have a two-fold purpose, a three-fold strategy, and a four-fold power. This explanation is not intended to explain the symbolic meaning of the beast's appearance in John's visions, but rather to aid our understanding.

First, the two-fold purpose:

1. Erase every footprint of Jesus Christ on Earth and replace Him with the Antichrist.

2. Demand worship of the Antichrist and the invisible dragon (Satan) that empowers him.

This two-fold purpose is accomplished through a potent three-fold strategy to turn people from Christ to Antichrist worshippers:

1. Lure people by offering pleasure, prosperity, power, and fame to win them over.

2. Deceive them through false miracles or teachings.

3. Persecute those who resist, punishing them with suffering and death.

Last, the dragon (Satan) and the beast (Antichrist) execute their three-fold strategy through a core four-fold power system:

1. Enticement

2. Economic control

3.   Religious influence

4.   Political power

To understand life under the Satanic ruler, think of Shadrach, Meshach, and Abednego in Babylon when Nebuchadnezzar set up the golden image and demanded that the entire world under his control worship it. Babylon will return, and it will be even more devastating this time. People will face a choice like no other: worship the Antichrist for earthly prosperity but eternal doom or worship Christ and face persecution and death. Figure 6 illustrates this human dilemma.

Figure 6: Unprecedented Human Dilemma
Antichrist or Christ?

Choosing Allegiance
Who Will You Worship?

Antichrist   **Christ**

Receives the Mark   Has God's Seal

Temporary Prosperity   Fierce Persecution

Final Place: Lake of Fire   Final Place: Heaven

As we've explored the bleak reality of life under the Antichrist's global empire, the significance of the mysterious number 666 and its mark has become increasingly apparent. In the next chapter, "Cracking the Code: Deciphering the Meaning of 666," we will uncover the hidden meaning behind this number through biblical numerology, prophecies, and ancient texts.

DECIPHERING
THE MEANING OF 666

What do ancient number systems, cryptic prophecies, and the Antichrist have in common? The answer may surprise you.

Unlocking the enigma of 666, a cryptic number intrinsically linked to the Antichrist, requires delving into the ancient practice of assigning numerical values to letters, ultimately revealing the identity of this vile figure and shedding light on the prophecy.

THE BIBLICAL FACTS FIRST

Getting the biblical facts is essential before interpretation. The Bible mentions 666 in the end-times context only in Revelation 13:18:

"This calls for wisdom: let the one who has understanding calculate the number of the beast, for it is the number of a man, and his number is 666."

(REVELATION 13:18, ESV)

Here are a few important facts from this verse:

- Understanding the number requires wisdom or some special knowledge.

- The number must be calculated (see gematria below). However, some scholars suggest that the Greek word for "calculate" in this context could also mean "figure out" or "come to understand."

- 666 is the number of the name of the beast. The Antichrist's name had a numerical value (Revelation 13:17).

- The number is six hundred sixty-six, not three sixes.

- 666 represents a man, a figure that embodies defiant humanity. Some scholars believe that the absence of the word "a" before "man" in the Greek grammar suggests that the number may refer to humanity rather than an individual.

- The term "number" appears thrice in that single verse, emphasizing its importance.

- John wrote Revelation in Greek, but the language of the Antichrist's name used for numeric symbolism is unclear (Greek, Hebrew, or even Latin?).

- Some ancient manuscripts use 616 instead of 666. Most scholars agree 616 is likely a later editorial change. The original number John wrote about is 666, not 616.

With these facts, we can now review how Christians have interpreted the significance of 666.

TWO SYSTEMS OF INTERPRETATION

No theme in the Bible has sparked the imagination and speculation of God's people like 666. However, most interpretations fall under one of two groups: symbolic or historical.

SYMBOLIC INTERPRETATION

In this view, 666 is a symbolic number that represents defiant humanity. As mentioned before, the absence of an article "a" or "the" before "man" in Revelation 13:18 supports this view. Looking beyond grammar, however, the context of Revelation 13 and other Bible passages support an individual—a coming prince (Daniel 9:26); the man of sin (2 Thessalonians 2:3).

Furthermore, humanity does not have a secret name that requires special wisdom to understand. And why would John use numerical symbolism (gematria) to conceal the special name of humanity?

HISTORICAL VIEW

The historical view posits that 666 is the numeric value of a historical figure's name—past, present, or future. Although John likely had a figure in view when he wrote Revelation 13:17, the Scriptures still point to a future figure—the man of sin or the Satanic prince—yet to come. When that Satanic world ruler is revealed, his name, through gematria, will add up to 666.

So, what is gematria?

GEMATRIA OR ISOPSEPHY — NUMERICAL SYMBOLISM

Gematria (Hebrew) or isopsephy (Greek) is a system of assigning numbers to letters and then adding up the numbers to derive a total for a word or phrase. The number 666 is the sum of the numeric values of the letters of the Antichrist's name.

Though many might find it difficult to grasp in our modern culture, most ancient languages did not have numbers as we do today. Instead, they used the letters of their alphabet as numbers. For example, the Jews assigned numbers to the letters of the Hebrew alphabet as follows: aleph = 1, bet = 2, gimel = 3, etc.

Thus, every name can be converted to a number by summing the numerical values of its letters. Please see Figure 7 for an example of gematria applied to the name of Nero, the vile Roman emperor.

Figure 7: Decoding Numerical Symbolism
Gematria (Hebrew) Applied to Nero Caesar

Numeric Values of Hebrew Letters

1 = א	20 = כ	200 = ר
2 = ב	30 = ל	300 = ש
3 = ג	40 = מ	400 = ת
4 = ד	50 = נ	
5 = ה	60 = ס	
6 = ו	70 = ע	
7 = ז	80 = פ	
8 = ח	90 = צ	
9 = ט	100 = ק	
10 = י		

Application to the Name of Nero

"Nero Caesar" in Hebrew

נ	Nun	50
ר	Resh	200
ו	Waw	6
נ	Nun	50
ק	Quap	100
ס	Samekh	60
ר	Resh	200
		666

WHY GEMATRIA?

Why use a number instead of an alphabetic name? The answer lies in secrecy.

Using the number of someone's name can hide their identity from some while revealing it to others. A notable example, famous among Bible scholars, is a love story quoted by the German theologian Adolf Deissmann, written on the walls of Pompeii (an ancient city in what is now Italy): "I love her whose number is 545."

This man openly professed his love for his beloved on a city wall, yet he concealed her identity from anyone who could read the text. Only the woman and those who knew the matter could decipher the person referenced in the writing. We can imagine the smile on that woman's face each time she read that public message while others remained oblivious.

When John wrote 666 in Revelation 13:18, he likely had a contemporary ruler in mind. Using gematria, he hid the ruler's name from some and unveiled it to those with understanding.

SO WHAT DOES 666 REPRESENT?

In Revelation 13:18, 666 is the sum of the numerical values of the letters of the Antichrist's name. John likely had a specific ruler in mind and used gematria or isopsephy to hide the name while revealing it only to those who could understand it.

Most scholars agree that Nero's name in Hebrew adds up to 666. But a future ruler is coming; his name will add up to 666. God alone knows if the language used for the number of his name will be Hebrew, Greek, Latin, or something else, even English!

Christians who know this verse and are on Earth during the Antichrist's reign will have no problem understanding 666 and its present application. But I pray that none of us reading this book will be left behind to meet the Antichrist and explain the meaning of 666 to others should these events occur in our time.

As we delve further into the enigma of 666 and the identity of the Antichrist, one essential piece of the puzzle remains: the mark of the beast. This symbol represents allegiance to the Antichrist and has profound implications for the fate of humanity during the end times. In the next chapter, "The Mark Revealed: Unmasking the Beast's Ultimate Symbol," we will uncover the hidden truths behind this mark and explore its far-reaching consequences. Are you ready to learn the secrets behind the mark that will change the world forever?

UNMASKING THE BEAST'S ULTIMATE SYMBOL

Symbols have held immense power throughout history, yet none rival the mark of the beast, which will determine the destinies of countless souls.

After exploring the significance of 666 in identifying the Antichrist, our investigation delves deeper into the heart of darkness to uncover its true nature. This chapter will reveal the beast's ultimate emblem, exposing its dual purpose and devastating consequences for its bearers.

THE BIBLICAL FACTS FIRST

The phrase "mark of the beast" is found solely in Revelation, with the crucial passage in Revelation 13:16–17:

It causes all to be marked on the right hand or the forehead,
so that no one can buy or sell unless he has the mark, that is,
the name of the beast or the number of its name.

(REVELATION 13:16–17)

- The Greek word for "mark" is *charagma*, which denotes a concavity produced by engraving, etching, branding, cutting, imprinting, or stamping.

- Outside of Revelation, *charagma* appears once in the New Testament in Acts 17:29, referring to an image created by art.

- The mark was given to everyone, regardless of social status.

- The mark was placed on the right hand or forehead.

- The mark was required for buying or selling—thus carrying significant commercial and economic implications.

- The mark can take the form of the Antichrist's name or the number of his name.

- The mark of the beast essentially represents the name of the beast in alphabetic letters or numbers.

- The Bible does not detail the exact nature of the mark but shows it will bear the name of the beast in either of its two forms.

- Although not explicitly stated, the Bible implies the mark as a permanent condition that cannot be removed or reversed.

- Those who receive the mark will experience prosperity during the Antichrist's reign but will ultimately be marked for God's wrath and the lake of fire.

Armed with these biblical facts, let's revisit the crucial concept of symbolism mentioned earlier.

BIBLICAL SYMBOLISM AND THE MARK OF THE BEAST

Given the significance of biblical symbolism in this context, it is essential to examine it in greater detail than previously noted. We will explore this in a two-step process: prophetic vision and symbolic interpretation.

THE PROPHETIC VISION

Symbolism originates from the vision received from God. The seer does not choose or invent the symbols in their mind; rather, God determines what the seer sees. In Revelation 13, John saw a terrifying creature with seven heads and people bearing marks on their foreheads and right hands. After seeing these symbols, he had to discern their meaning.

THE SYMBOLIC INTERPRETATION

Prophetic symbols in visions represent real-life people, places, events, objects, or periods. Our challenging task is to determine the meanings of these symbols, if they are indeed symbols.

An invaluable interpretive aid in Revelation is when God explicitly clarifies the meaning of symbols. For example, Jesus informed John that the seven lampstands he saw symbolized the seven churches (Revelation 1:20). Similarly, the dragon in John's visions represented Satan— an invisible spirit being on Earth in real life.

Hence, when John observed marks on people's heads and right hands in his vision, he saw a mark on their bodies. But was that mark a symbol of something, or was it a literal bodily mark in real life? If it was a symbol, what did it represent?

As expected, various interpretations of the mark have emerged.

FOUR COMMON INTERPRETATIONS OF THE MARK

What did the original readers of Revelation understand? Bible scholars have identified four plausible explanations (see Figure 8):

1. A tattoo or branding on the arm of insubordinate slaves and captured soldiers.

2. An imperial seal that bore the image and name of the Roman emperor.

3. The image and name of the Roman emperor on Roman coins.

4. Jewish phylacteries—small leather boxes containing Scriptures worn on the forehead and left hand.

Figure 8: Four Common Interpretations of the
Mark of the Beast
During the Time of Revelation's Writing

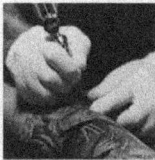

BODILY MARKS

Tattoos or branding of
insubrodinate slaves or
captured soldiers

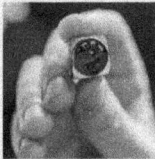

IMPERIAL SEALS

With the image and
name of the emperor

ROMAN COINS

Bearing the name and
image of the emperor

**JEWISH
PHYLACTERIES**

Small boxes with scriptures
worn on the forehead
and left arm

Regardless of what the mark might have meant to these first readers of John's letter, the key issue is the future manifestation of the mark when the Antichrist rises to power.

WHAT WOULD THE MARK BE IN THE ANTICHRIST'S GOVERNMENT?

Most Bible scholars agree that the mark John saw in the vision is symbolic; it represents allegiance, ownership, or control. However, that is only one aspect of the matter— the spiritual side. The Bible shows that the mark determined who could buy or sell. The buying and selling in this context are likely not symbolic activities but actual transactions.

Thus, the mark of the beast will be used in the marketplace to identify who can and cannot buy or sell. This identification system implies the mark will have some physical expression, something businesses and government officials can use to distinguish individuals, ensuring compliance with the Antichrist's government regulations.

So, the mark has two components: a spiritual aspect and a physical expression.

THE SPIRITUAL MARK

The mark of the beast is first a spiritual symbol. Revelation provides an excellent example of such a spiritual mark.

In Revelation 14:1, after discussing the mark of the beast in Revelation 13:16–18, John wrote that God has His name on His people's foreheads. Though he does not explicitly use the term "mark," the idea is the same: God has His own mark, called a "seal" in Revelation, on His people's foreheads.

Consequently, as the beast marks his followers on their foreheads, God seals His worshippers to signify their allegiance to Him.

THE PHYSICAL MARK

The spiritual mark, symbolizing allegiance and ownership, will have a physical expression. Regardless of the mark's precise physical nature, its purpose remains consistent: to identify those who worship the Antichrist.

We do not know what this physical mark will be. However, when the Antichrist reveals it, he will probably use existing systems to identify his loyal followers. Observe how the world functions today and consider how easy it will be to determine who can buy or sell, in-person or online.

Figure 9 summarizes the two dimensions of the mark:

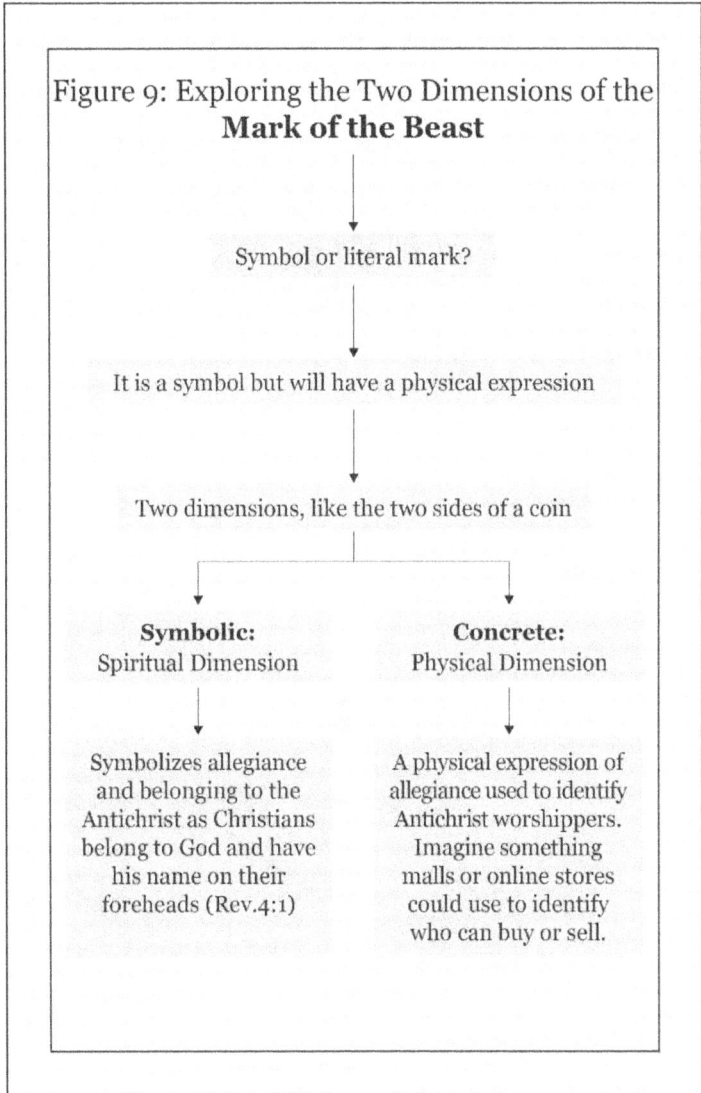

Figure 9: Exploring the Two Dimensions of the **Mark of the Beast**

Symbol or literal mark?

It is a symbol but will have a physical expression

Two dimensions, like the two sides of a coin

Symbolic: Spiritual Dimension	**Concrete:** Physical Dimension
Symbolizes allegiance and belonging to the Antichrist as Christians belong to God and have his name on their foreheads (Rev.4:1)	A physical expression of allegiance used to identify Antichrist worshippers. Imagine something malls or online stores could use to identify who can buy or sell.

As we have delved into the grave reality of the mark of the beast and its profound implications for the world, it is easy to become overwhelmed with fear and anxiety. However, not everything we hear or read about the number 666 and the mark of the beast is accurate. In the next chapter, "Dispelling Shadows: Confronting Fears and Debunking Myths about 666," we will address these fears, separating fact from fiction and clarifying the misconceptions that have clouded our understanding.

CONFRONTING FEARS AND DEBUNKING MYTHS ABOUT 666

Let us unravel the web of myths and fears surrounding the mark of the beast and 666. After examining the significance of the number and mark in previous chapters, we discovered many potential misconceptions.

In this chapter, we aim to dispel those gray areas, confront unwarranted fears, and debunk myths associated with 666 and the mark of the beast. But first, we'll begin by addressing a major problem associated with the study of end-time prophecies today: the pressure to predict.

THE PRESSURE TO IDENTIFY THE ANTICHRIST OR THE MARK OF THE BEAST BEFORE THE APPOINTED TIME

The Antichrist (the beast) and his mark will be revealed at a time set by God (2 Thessalonians 2:8). Any attempts to predict the identity of this Antichrist or the exact physical expression of the mark of the beast are attempts to do what God has not permitted us to do and will ultimately prove to be wrong.

As we have seen in the prior chapters, we can understand 666, the mark of the beast, and the book of Revelation without plunging into end-times prophecy speculations. We can understand 666 without any pressure to predict or speculate.

We must know the signs of the times and be aware of what is happening around us, but avoid attempting to go beyond God's limits.

FALSE ALARMS AND BOYCOTTS

In major global crises, some Christians will attempt to identify an Antichrist with a corresponding mark of the beast, as apocalyptic writings usually emerge during troubled times. The list of what believers have labeled as the mark is extensive: US Social Security numbers, barcodes, credit and electronic banking cards, microchip implants, and even the COVID-19 vaccine.

These claims, attempting to predict the mark before its time, raise false alarms, instill fear, and cause Christians sometimes to behave irrationally. Acknowledging the significant impact these claims can have on people's faith and conduct is crucial.

Interestingly, when the Antichrist appears, he might use one or more of these items to identify his followers. He could use microchip implants and cell phones alike. Should we stop using cell phones or abhor technology because the Antichrist will use them when he is ruling? We do not avoid the mark primarily by avoiding physical objects but by believing in Christ and holding on to our faith in Him.

False alarms raise fears among Christians, afraid of mistakenly taking this mark. But can a Christian unknowingly receive the mark of the beast?

CHRISTIANS CANNOT UNKNOWINGLY RECEIVE THE MARK OF THE BEAST

The mark of the beast symbolizes pledged loyalty with a physical expression, making it impossible to receive it by mistake. A Christian cannot accidentally receive the mark, just as a sinner cannot accidentally become born again.

Worshippers of the beast will knowingly entrust their lives to the Antichrist—by free will or government compulsion—just as we entrust our lives to Jesus intentionally and willfully by faith. The physical expression is an outward manifestation of an internal, destiny-sealing mark.

Most fears of accidentally receiving the mark through implanted chips, vaccines, or barcodes are biblically unfounded. A proper understanding of the Scriptures should dispel these fears and concerns.

THE MARK IS A PHYSICAL MARK ON THE BODY

The Bible has not revealed the exact nature of the mark. Until the Antichrist is revealed, we will not know whether his mark will be a physical object or mark on the body, such as a microchip, or an external object, such as a special card with a barcode.

As mentioned earlier, the mark is not primarily a physical mark but a sign of pledged allegiance to worship the Antichrist and Satan. However, it will have a physical expression, a kind of government ID.

Though Jesus Christ wants us to know the signs of the times, He has not given us the job of speculating on things He has purposefully concealed until the right time.

THE ANTICHRIST WILL TRY TO FORCE THE MARK ON EVERYONE

Some believe the mark will be forcibly given to everyone during the Antichrist's reign. However, the Bible states people will have a choice to accept or reject it.

If the Antichrist cannot win allegiance through prosperity and pleasure, he will attempt persuasion through false miracles and teachings, claiming to be the true Christ. If unsuccessful, he will persecute offenders and use the death penalty to force the living to receive the mark. They must willingly worship him and receive a government ID to access his regime's pleasures and prosperity.

Regardless of his tactics, one thing remains clear: the Antichrist cannot apply the mark to people without their consent. He will not order his agents to roam the streets, marking as many people as they encounter. Instead, individuals will accept it willingly or under coercion that compels them to comply.

Please see Figure 10 for a summary of six common misconceptions about the mark of the beast.

Figure 10: Six Common Misconceptions and Errors to Avoid Regarding **666 and the Mark of the Beast**

1. Attempting to predict the identify of the coming antichrist or the exact nature of the mark before the time God has set.

2. Assuming the sole objective of studying 666 or the mark of the beast is to identify the antichrist or the mark of the beast.

3. Fears of unintentionally receiving the mark of the beast at work or from the government.

4. The mark is thought of to be primarily a bodily physical mark.

5. Unfounded fears of using certain objects or technology due to false claims that they are the mark of the beast.

6. Attempts to seek to know what God has intentionally withheld until the due time.

This concise book cannot list all the misconceptions about 666 and the mark of the beast, nor is it desirable or feasible to do so. However, the examples above make the point: We live when the signs of the end appear everywhere, and we cannot ignore or pretend not to notice them. In our next and final chapter, we will explore how Christians can live in the end times, anticipating Jesus's return, overcoming the wicked one, and being neither frightened nor deceived.

HOW TO LIVE IN THE END TIMES

The ultimate showdown: will the Second Coming of Christ or the coming reign of the Antichrist define how today's believers live their lives?

Having dispelled the shadows, fears, and misconceptions surrounding 666 and the mark of the beast, we now shift our focus to the Bible's empowering message for those navigating these tumultuous times. This chapter will explore practical insights for thriving in the end times without being troubled, fearful, or fainthearted.

TWO GROUPS OF END-TIMES CHRISTIANS

Since Jesus left, Christians have commonly thought He would return in their generation, especially during major catastrophic world events. Our generation is almost certain

Jesus will return in our time—with unprecedented moral decadence, political unrest, economic turmoil, plagues, and natural disasters.

Chronologically, we can categorize Christians in these last days into two groups: those living before the Antichrist's reign and those present during his rule. For example, although we are in the end times, we have not yet entered the era of the Antichrist. Most Christians believe the rapture will take place before the Antichrist's reign. Other Christians, however, have different views on this.

This book follows the pre-tribulation view that the church will be raptured before the Antichrist unleashes hell on Earth. Therefore, despite the multiple signs of the end, God's prophetic clock for the end time has not yet started ticking. We are still in the pre-tribulation, pre-rapture generation.

So how should we live?

LIVING IN THE END TIMES BEFORE THE ANTICHRIST

Here are two explicit commandments for living in the end times:

1. Live with the constant expectation of Jesus's return.

   Christians should always be ready for Christ's return, and that sense of His imminent coming will make us live in holiness and do His work quickly (1 John 3:3).

2. Overcome the dragon and the beasts.

   We should overcome the dragon (Satan), his workers, and his devices as we wait.

Anticipating Christ's return and overcoming the devil requires us to recognize the signs of the times and remain informed about global events. The continuous struggles in everyday Christian living and the intensifying darkness in the world serve as reminders that the sinister dragon is already present and active.

THE DRAGON AND THE BEAST TODAY

When reading the book of Revelation, particularly chapter 12, some Christians may be tempted to think that Satan, depicted as the seven-headed dragon, will appear on Earth during the last days. However, this is a grave mistake.

That dragon, Satan, is here on Earth right now. In fact, he has been here since Adam and Eve fell in the Garden. Some of us may be shocked to learn that the dragon may have attacked us today, attempting to seduce us into disobeying God, just as he seduced Eve.

The dragon is already here, constantly working to fulfill his two-fold purpose through a three-fold strategy and a four-fold power system mentioned earlier. He is actively seeking to turn people from Christ to Satan. He lures them with promises of pleasure, power, or fame and through other temptations and lies. How many Christians have shipwrecked their faith because of the promise of pleasure, power, fame, prosperity, or celebrity status?

Satan's false prophets are deceiving many with false teachings and miracles today. And his antichrist leaders are persecuting Christians all over the world.

Therefore, it is crucial to acknowledge the simple but profound truth that the dragon is already here, and his antichrists and false prophets are hard at work. However, there will come a time when this work will expand on a global scale, surpassing anything previously witnessed. And the coming Antichrist will fully embody everything antichrist, and his false prophet will fully embody everything false prophet.

As a result, here is Jesus's command for us today: Overcome the dragon and his beastly activities. Do not reject Christ for sexual pleasure or the promise of prosperity, fame, or power gained through ungodly lifestyles. Be discerning about what you hear from pastors, teachers, or prophets, and stand firm in your faith, even amid persecution.

HOW TO AVOID THE MARK OF THE BEAST

There is no mark of the beast to avoid until the beast appears and reveals his Satanic government ID. Believers in Jesus Christ during the Antichrist's reign must profess their faith in Jesus and reject the Antichrist, even at the cost of their lives.

However, for Christians living before this time, there is no mark of the beast to avoid until the beast rises to power. The mark is not yet here. However, we have the dragon, the spirit of the Antichrist, and satanic pressures all around us.

There are two things people can do today to overcome the dragon, his beasts, and his activities:

1. Believe in Jesus as Savior and Lord.

2. Maintain a healthy relationship with Him every day.

So here is how to overcome the dragon in these perilous times before the Antichrist and his government: resist temptations, avoid false teachers and prophets, and do not bow to persecution in any form.

THE MISERABLE DEFEAT OF THE DRAGON AND THE BEAST

In the darkness of these end-time events, two events shine a bright light:

1. The pitiful end of the dragon and the Beast.

2. The believer's entrance into unfathomable eternal glory.

John presents the end of the dragon, the Antichrist, and the false prophet:

> *"And the devil who had deceived them was thrown into the lake of fire and sulfur where the beast and the false prophet were, and they will be tormented day and night forever and ever."*
>
> (REVELATION 20:10)

Paul puts it this way:

"And then the lawless one will be revealed, whom the Lord Jesus will kill with the breath of his mouth and bring to nothing by the appearance of his coming."

(2 THESSALONIANS 2:8)

Jesus will defeat and destroy the Antichrist. (Please see the graphic depiction below.)

Afterward, Christians will receive their full inheritance from God, including a new spiritual body that can fully contain and express the Holy Spirit without limitations from sin, the flesh, or physical weakness. God will fully immerse our being with the fullness of His Being, allowing us to live—feel, think, act, and speak—as He does.

It is impossible to fully describe the joy and glory that await those who have put their faith in Jesus Christ as their Savior and Lord. Nothing in this world can compare to the eternal bliss that awaits them, and none of its troubles or fleeting pleasures are worth forfeiting such priceless glory.

Rather than fear what is happening in the world, our hearts resonate with the words of John:

> *"He who testifies to these things says, 'Surely I am coming quickly.' Amen. Even so, come, Lord Jesus."*
>
> (REVELATION 22:20, KJV)

CONCLUSION

Congratulations! You have just completed a crash course on Eschatology!

At the heart of what we've learned is this: Six hundred sixty-six, or 666, is the numerical value of the Antichrist's name used to identify him, while the mark of the Beast is a spiritual mark with a tangible manifestation employed to distinguish the Antichrist's loyal worshippers.

Our journey to this understanding has been straightforward. We established a proper context and then used aids to help us comprehend the relevant Scripture verses.

Having examined the Antichrist and his beastly global government, we decoded 666 using gematria and unveiled the dual components of the mark—spiritual and physical. Next, we addressed several common errors and misconceptions, especially the pressure to predict end-time events. Finally, we explored how to navigate these challenging times, even before the Antichrist takes center stage.

The dragon is already present and at work, diligently preparing to set up his global government. Don't let the dragon and his allies steal your heart from Jesus: be cautious of worldly pleasures; remain vigilant against false teachers and prophets; and stand strong in the face of persecution.

Here is God's command for us during these troubling days:

"Arise, shine, for your light has come, and the glory of the Lord has risen upon you. For behold, darkness shall cover the earth, and thick darkness the peoples; but the Lord will arise upon you, and His glory will be seen upon you."

(ISAIAH 60:1–2)

A PERSONAL NOTE FROM DR. OBEN

Thank you for reading "666: The Mark of the Beast Made Simple." Your feedback is invaluable. If this book was insightful or helpful, please consider leaving an honest review on Amazon. Your thoughts not only help me improve but may also help other believers gain a deeper understanding of this subject and live free of fear, worry, or deception in the last days.

Sharing your experience can make a significant difference for those seeking to understand 666 and the mark of the beast in these troubling times.

Thank you for your support, and may God's love and grace continue to shine upon you and your loved ones.

Warm regards,
Dr. Oben

FREE MINI E-BOOKS

Deshen Mini E-books, published by Patrick Oben Ministries, offer concise yet impactful excerpts of the Word designed to create profound transformation. These e-books present deep biblical truths in a reader-friendly format. Each mini e-book is crafted to be read in just 10 to 15 minutes, ensuring a swift, transformative experience through an encounter with the Holy Spirit in the Scriptures.

- Keys to Open Your Spiritual Eyes: Discover Two Ways God Opens Your Eyes and Five Steps to Facilitate His Intervention

- How to Receive Rhema: Learn 9 Powerful Insights to Enhance Your Ability to Hear God's Voice Instantly

- The Devotional Life of Jesus: Find Inspiration and Encouragement for Daily Communion with the Father

QUESTIONS?

You might have questions about some themes covered in this book or need clarity on some topics only briefly discussed. If so, please contact me directly using my email address below:

patrick@patrickoben.com

Also, please visit our website, which has over two thousand articles and devotionals to encourage, strengthen, and build up your spiritual life. Here is a link to our website:

www.patrickoben.com

ABOUT THE AUTHOR

D r. Patrick Oben is a dedicated internal medicine physician and the founder of Patrick Oben Ministries, Inc. His teaching ministry focuses on helping believers develop essential skills, such as accurate Scripture interpretation and cultivating an intimate relationship with the Holy Spirit.

Balancing his dual passions, Dr. Oben cares for people's physical well-being through medical practice while nurturing their spiritual growth through his gift of wisdom and skill in teaching. Besides his clinical work, he contributes his medical insights as an Editorial Review Board member for the respected *Journal of Patient Experience.*

As a keen Bible student and teacher, Dr. Oben examines Scriptures and theological resources with a physician's precision. He is skilled in distilling complex biblical truths into clear, relatable insights. Dr. Oben lives in Ankeny, Iowa, with his wife, Maayuk, and their three beloved children.